Speak, Shade

Speak, Shade
Copyright © 2013 Raymond Gibson
Paperback ISBN: 978-0-9840352-2-9

All rights reserved: except for the purpose of quoting brief passages for review, no part of this book may be reproduced or transmitted in any form or by any means, electronic or mechanical, including photocopying, recording, or by any information storage and retrieval system, without permission in writing from the publisher.

Cover art: Pd Lietz
Interior art: Lucretious
Cover design: Steven Asmussen
Design & Layout: Steven Asmussen

Glass Lyre Press, LLC.
P.O. Box 2693
Glenview, IL 60026

www.GlassLyrePress.com

Speak, Shade

Poems by
Raymond Gibson

Somos contos contando contos. Nada.
   —*Ricardo Reis*

Contents

The Cataracts	11
Echo of Light	12
Distances	13
Hand in Emptiness	14
Blind River	15
Sculpture Garden	16
Surfacing	17
Peregrination	18
Mene Mene Tekel Parsin	19
Keep The Light On	20
The Moirai	21
Twilight Song	22
Calendar	23
Cardinal Senses	24
Sabachthani	25
The Unrequital	27
The Night Shore	28
If	29
Galatea	30
Nocturne	31
The Voyeur	32
Hic Sunt	33
Against Futility	34
Fiat	35
Light Is God's Shadow	36
Blink	38
Blind Timescapes	39
Notes	40

The Cataracts

What is it what is it now

the delicate gauze flower
in the eye-socket
the dull orange of a shut eye in light

this could be anything
like the half-formed abstracts of a Bacon

butcher's fat a snake
or chains draped by feathers
the focus can't hold

and now
fingernails tile the walls

I glance at my hands expecting
red absences
what are the eyes if not complicit

not a glass shield but the holes of a mask

Echo of Light

As though you had fallen
into a well
and the senses jettison

the sense of movement
passed so long
you doubt the bottom rushing up

the eyes forget open from shut
in the unshifting black reply

but it was a dreamless sleep
nothing more
the same face tearing loose from gravity
the mirror catching your breath

yes here is light
though the star's years dead

Distances

෮

How describe sight to the blind
we begin

but how to talk in the black
vacuity of space
the words can't carry

it is light
and beyond it opaqueness

how explain
to a four-fingered man
absence
without a knuckle or stump

to tell is to amputate the very digit

what we have we lose
a richness in bones
a poise astride crumbling pedestals

what we see we never have

Hand in Emptiness

To live in a winding sheet of skin
is to be separate

to pour through crowds without
glancing brush
is to live ghostly as water

but the touch of skin to skin
it startles the sleepwalker

to know loss
is to first know possession

to feel the smooth and human nape
one hungers for the solid edge
beyond burning nerve

but to touch once once
weaves a cage of fire

loneliness we never knew

Blind River

☙

Why do we go on have we an obligation to the dead those who came before always said

---

Dark times lay ahead

And they marched toward the future hoping a few generations would buffer them from the vague doom to come

---

Still they bore sons and whispered that their small age would not see the chaos yet

---

Cowards sending children ahead of them in the dark

Sculpture Garden

∽

The eyeless bust of a god without mouth the wishing-cage strewn with keys the fountain-hand nails cut to the quick the hung chains that sway fire-lit the bronze curtain drawn on a wall the two arms and fig-leaf on pedestal and the end an installation none can enter nor see at all

Surfacing

ॐ

The air resists my movement like water it is late doors are closing blue night wells in the room the way warmth retracts through the seams I sit on the bed's edge shadows spread from the corners they wrap me like a veil and shawl as tepid sweat pools in my ear and the dream flits from leaves to moths to ash and I am left if I am with dampness to skin a faint taste of metals intangible silence within

Peregrination

෧ඞ

Touch is the sense when objects meet and
sight that anticipates touch

look a deaf-mute leading the blind by hand

both are neither ghosts nor memories but
ourselves at a dream's mercy

here in the gateless fence of horn and ivory

Mene Mene Tekel Parsin

☙

To number to weigh to divide always
cursed with the next-to-best

a gray heart snow-of-ash these ashlars
an empty mirror I reflect on
names make men take things lightly

death's pollen and a lake of ice

this sky echoes in stumps
the drowned the rootward trees

they have sold what is we buy what isn't

in an old purse jangle
one hundred twenty-six shekels
thirty will kill a god

and the boat-ride to hell isn't free

Keep The Light On

I keep my last breath in an empty cage
        and half a bronzed
    heart crammed with cigarette ends
the light bourbon | the silence unnerving

I keep my last teeth a set of blank dice
        and both hollowed
    jaws a roulette dial to tell the time
the light bourbon | my speech burdened

I keep my last blood wound skin-tight
        and twin purblind
    eyes red-webbed in a purple night
the light burning | these thoughts moths

The Moirai

☙

Just as a guitar with braided strings
    will not snap but cannot play, just as
        death's tremolo gnaws with shears,
            given space is woven lines, a loom,

        a harp, and we notes that vibrate
      cannot help but ride its wave, given
the absolute swallows its numbers
    as it does its stars, it follows that

        we are but movement, all phantoms
          before fingers of shadow, follows
        that catgut and ivory spin our fiber,
    therefore, we should dance as atoms

unless we've no partner nor feet,
    we should behave as music unless
        the mean of noises is silence, then
            octaves thread a web in deaf night,

        our fuse burns yet we give no light,
    our spark hums in a mute key along
a strand of brittle hair, and vacuum
    claims sound goes as far as breath,

        this breath takes us to the next, red
            sinews bind and stretch on chimes,
        a mosaic of bone, the carpet weave
    of nerve with bow strings of blood

floods with white noise concrete
    as a shriek, a cry which brings us
        back to the stitched ear, the wand,
            the strings unraveling in the wind

Twilight Song

There sinister doves
wail for a name
and I scatter like red embers

there dexterous owls
demand a name
and I smolder like a lantern

between dog and wolf
a name congeals
as I weep like a tallow candle

for the sleep of poppies lilies

Calendar

☙

A ring with thirty keys that try
the lock and repeat and repeat

Cardinal Senses

࿇

This number will not do

what of the senses of movement and time
and lacklove that pain
we fill with which does not answer
to either of five wounds

what of the visible silence of a blank page
that scrawled on
speaks only its volute of ink

is it nobler
the tattoo of a metered heart

than Damoclean time
which drips its gall from haft
to blade to mouth

we've water for blood now
the farther we drift
the more likely we'll freeze

and eight chambers shatter in expanse of ice

14 February 2004

Sabachthani
for Brandywine Sejeck

☙

I in the canopic jar of my flesh
   in the egg of bone ask you
love what is it   We two parted
   by the space from this page
to the cloistered eye dreaming
   can share no answers
If I dove my hand into this
   ossuary of broken sentences
I'd dredge a different sense
   If our eyes met languageless
the worded scroll of a glance
   would lie burn between them

Say love is the want to cross
   the void and not the crossing
There is no bridge neither
   hair-breadth nor blade-sharp
threaded from skull to skull
   but cold atomic collision
a sowing of salt stars on
   the black vault of grave sky
It is a gravity without motion
   a motion without touch
touch that can hold no closer
   though bodies overlap below

We forsaken together like grapes
   huddled separate in cluster
must bear our dry-sweetness as if
   it were love   Let the pelvis
unhinge like snake jaws   Let
   the coccyx uncurl like a tongue
The makers gather start and part
   while the babe glazed with

the brood of the heart wells
　　with vipers and milk　Ours
the pensive child that will gather
　　part with others lonely as us

The Unrequital

Our pain skirts both nerve and skin
it is all we grasp of warmth's touch

this dull flame in the marrow
that shivers its cells
the red suns arc to a throbbing thread
which courses each vein

then blatant noon
thirst yearning thirst
otherwise we are numb

we are eyes within
eyes
we were each other's cynosure

now I am beneath you
as mute stars above

woman you have cleft my days in two

The Night Shore

Somniloquies rise like the drowned their
    lungfuls of air ripple as
        indecipherable

a vision translucent as halite in opaque
    huelessness the night of it
        meandering

breath is the sea rote I float to the pupil
    wade the green iris shut
        in its eyelid

these thoughts dream me and not I them
    how from out of silence
        clarities swim

If
for Timothy Guyah
☙

The congruity of a chess table to the chequered floor it stands on and the broken symmetry of the pieces midgame

---

The similarity of pawns to bedposts and sleeping to dying coupled with the ironies that the dead are cordoned off to graveyards while death roams free and that headboards and headstones resemble each other

---

The way statues are called lifelike and the living statuesque the way life mask and death mask are synonyms

---

The ivory of knights and the bone of dice at cross purposes in the same ebony hand and the interchangeability of one hand for another in a game made greater than the sum of its players

---

That vitiligo startles the manner in which maps change and whether society's board contains gray squares when played from memory

---

The game being a metonym for civilization and a metaphor for war that the two are not mutually exclusive

---

Whether chess becomes a solitaire variant on the heavenly level and a migraine aura at the universal

---

How neither model nor conceit lasts

Galatea

೫⊃

What scared her still was the myth that the body reposed like stone in its final attitude but when told the truth that even the last rigor fades the statue moved

Nocturne

☙

Take the night it's yours while the light drains from the house this sky still has its stars come each way is right if every use seems wasted there is no misspent time and though the stars keep to their arc they remain as bright

The Voyeur

He walks through the gallery
with a drapery of flesh tied to bone
and legs of dull pipes
to stop here before a painting
The Lovers

gripping one another by the forearms
they crowd their pale breasts
in whose blue shadows the snowy hills
rise like

      a winter landscape
where two white leopards
sink fangs into the other's neck
never to end the bite
for the mortal jump of blood staved by tooth

yet there are no cats but growls
his ribs guard

the two holding themselves for warmth
have no need of him
and they will never freeze

they are not real there is no gallery

only the hallway of a poem
and on the floor
by a mirror a discarded curtain and flutes

Hic Sunt
Paradiso xxxiii

☙

There is no outside
the fascicle

for a book
to exist
there must be

paper press
a binder

room to open

the mind is a panicle
stemmed from
body

three rings one ring
three

how geometry
posits

a geometer

shaped shapes in
nature
to abstract

we live in the ink
of nerve

intact

Against Futility

A knife of glass slicing at water
hands of water grasping at sand

      a quartz stylus and tablet of ice

wake of dust and windfall ciphers
a snowflake language that scrolls

      the ink is clear and dries blank

dreams spill into wakefulness as
a trickle roots through its stone

      the book not yet felled planted

Fiat

☙

Let there be

as if we were

born into it as if
the eye were
a cave

brevis a spark
in the geode we inhabit

amethyst stalactites
glint
like stars

the moth-eaten holes

in the taut black
shawl

space looms

the widow Sophia
weaves on

Light Is God's Shadow

ஐ

 First there
  were
 shadows

    though there was
    nothing

 to cast them

    and no light

 light had
a name before
   it
 existed

    a name
    like
    a shadow nothing
    cast

and there nothing
  stood
 and said light

    the spark
    of
    which shone
    on
    the shadows

 then something
  came
 to stand

                    between light
                    and
                    the shadows

      cast
   and erect
         as
   reflections

                    as if water
                    had
                    stood

   like a heatless
         flame

                    between smoke
                    and a gleam

      it was life

                    the
                    twin dreams

Blink

ଛୀ

They emerge
finish

the red door
of birth

and the light
of two
windows
dwindle

the words
diverge
and merge

diminish

as any white can
kindle
will perish

or mark
how the dark
drinks all

at the brink

things look
small and say
less

Blind Timescapes

☙

which pass under fingertips the comatose
interred in memory a cruor
of ichor

reason's dreaming creates monsters

the divine
masks the unknown

this ubiquitous
silence of what no one told the audient
void undulant

breaths plash in the sky where I stood
my shadow stayed

ask for neither light nor place to stand

but to be awake with hands to take in this
the dark night and thread
the dawns

Notes

Mene Mene Tekel Parsin — The title comes from Daniel five 126 shekels adds up the weight of coins from the title and note that the reflections do not match

Twilight Song — The mourning dove's call resembles the word who several times plaintively and line seven is a calque of entre chien et loup a French phrase for the darkest part of dusk

Cardinal Senses — Lines eleven through thirteen conflate the sword of Damocles with the Jewish angel of death's sword

Sabachthani — The title comes from the first verse of Psalm twenty-two in Aramaic

The Voyeur — Lines eleven through fourteen paraphrase a Kenneth Tynan description of a love affair from loose recollection

Fiat — The name Sophia means wisdom

Light Is God's Shadow — The poem plays off of Genesis and Plato once wrote Light is God's shadow

Blind Timescapes — Line four reworks Goya's quote El sueño de la razón produce monstruos and the dark night refers to that of the soul

Raymond Gibson graduated from the creative writing MFA program at Florida Atlantic University. He won first place in the Florida Community College Press Association Magazine Competition of 2003 for best poem. His work can be found in *Oak Bend Review*, the Tiny Truths section of *Creative Nonfiction*, *THIS Literary Magazine*, *Four and Twenty Poetry*, *Squawk Back*, *River Poets Journal*, and *Pirene's Fountain*. He currently lives in his hometown of Hollywood. Florida.

GLASS LYRE PRESS, LLC
"Exceptional works to replenish the spirit"

Poetry collections
Poetry chapbooks
Select short & flash fiction
Occasional anthologies

Glass Lyre Press is a small independent literary press interested in work which is technically accomplished and distinctive in style, as well as fresh in its approach and treatment. Glass Lyre seeks writers of diverse backgrounds who display mastery over the many areas of contemporary literature, writers with a powerful and dynamic aesthetic, and ability to stir the imagination and engage the emotions and intellect of a wide audience of readers.

The Glass Lyre vision is to connect the world through language and art. We hope to expand the scope of poetry and short fiction for the general reader through exceptionally well-written books which call forth our deepest emotions and thoughts, delight our senses, challenge our minds, and provide clarity, resonance and insight.

www.GlassLyrePress.com